Down on the Farm

SHEEP

Hannah Ray

QED Publishing

Copyright © QED Publishing 2006

First published in the UK in 2006 by
QED Publishing
A Quarto Group company
226 City Road
London ECIV 2TT
www.qed-publishing.co.uk

A Catalogue record for this book is available
from the British Library.

ISBN 1 84538 466 0

Written by Hannah Ray
Consultant Sally Morgan
Designed by Liz Wiffen
Editor Paul Manning
Picture Researcher Joanne Forrest Smith
Illustrations by Chris Davidson

Publisher Steve Evans
Editorial Director Jean Coppendale
Art Director Zeta Davies

Printed and bound in China

CONTENTS

Words in **bold** can be found in the Glossary on page 22.

Sheep on the farm

Do you know where we get wool for socks and jumpers to keep us warm in winter? Or the meat in tasty lamb chops? Or the soft leather to make coats, gloves and slippers? All these things come from sheep.

A mother sheep and her two young **lambs**.

FARM FACT
Did you know that counting sheep is supposed to make you feel sleepy? Try it and see!

Sheep are often kept in large groups called flocks.

Farmers all over the world keep sheep. Sheep give us wool, meat and milk. In Britain there are 44 million sheep, and in Australia and New Zealand there are more sheep than people!

5

Sheep from nose to tail

A fully grown sheep is about 80cm tall at the shoulder, and weighs up to 100kg. That's the same weight as five six-year-old children!

Eye

Ear

Thick, woolly fleece

Tail

Nose

Mouth

Foot with two toes; each toe ends in a hoof

Some sheep have horns that grow in curly, spiral shapes like this Scottish Blackface.

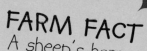

Height of six-year-old child

Height of sheep

FARM FACT
A sheep's horns are made of the same material as our fingernails.

It's a sheep's life...

A baby lamb grows inside its mother for five months before it is ready to be born.

For the first few weeks of its life, the lamb feeds on its mother's milk.

After two weeks, the lamb will start to nibble grass. At about six weeks old, it will start to eat hay and grain.

A baby lamb being fed by its mother.

At six months old, a female sheep can have a baby of her own, but most sheep are one and a half years old before they have their first lamb.

Sheep on a farm live for about 13 to 15 years.

Fleecy facts

A sheep's woolly coat is called a fleece. The sheep's fleece helps to keep it warm in winter.

In the spring, when the weather is warmer, the sheep's fleece is clipped off. The **shearers** are very **skilled** and shearing does not hurt the sheep.

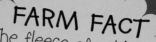

The fleece is washed and combed to straighten it. This is called carding. The fleece can then be **spun** into **yarn** to make the clothes we wear.

Wool being spun into yarn by machine.

11

Woolly wonders

Different breeds of sheep from around the world give us many kinds of wool.

The wool from these Scottish Blackface sheep is thick and rough. Carpets, mattresses and **tweed** are made from this wool.

Wool from these American Navajo sheep is used to make beautiful rugs and blankets.

FARM FACT
Even if your woolly jumper gets wet, it will still keep you warm! Wool is also strong and will last a long time.

The wool from Australian Merino sheep is used to make warm, woolly jumpers.

From mutton to make-up

Sheep give us many things as well as wool. Meat from a young sheep is called lamb. Meat from an older sheep is called mutton.

Sheep also give us very soft leather, called sheepskin. Sheepskin is used to make coats, boots and rugs. The woolly fleece is left on the back of the leather to make it extra warm and cosy.

FARM FACT
Sheep's milk is often used to make special cheeses. These Pecorino cheeses come from Italy.

Sheep even help to make candles and make-up! That is because candle wax and some make-up and skin creams contain lanolin, a natural oil that is found in the fleece of sheep.

15

Baa, baa, which sheep?

Lots of different types of sheep can be found all over the world.

MORADA NOVA

These sheep look a lot like goats. They are short-haired and come from Brazil.

MANX LOGHTAN

These sheep are from the Isle of Man. They can have two, four or even six horns!

RACKA

These sheep
from Hungary
are famous for
their horns.
The horns of
the male sheep
can be 60cm long.

WENSLEYDALE

These British sheep
have deep-bluish
faces, ears and legs.
They produce very
good wool.

Sheep customs

PERU

In June each year, the farmers of Cuzco in Peru dress up their sheep and take them to church to celebrate the festival of San Juan (Saint John).

NEW ZEALAND

In March, the world's biggest sheep-shearing contest is held in New Zealand. People compete to become 'Champion of the Golden Shears'!

ROMANIA

These colourful Romanian sheep are taking part in the Sambra Oilor festival, when villagers celebrate the flocks coming down from the mountains.

FARM FACT
In some countries, mules or llamas are used to scare off wild animals that might hurt or frighten the sheep.

Shoebox weaving

Weaving with sheep's wool is fun! All you need is a shoebox, string, some sticky tape and different-coloured lengths of wool.

1 Ask a grown-up to make cuts 1cm deep along the two short ends of a shoebox.

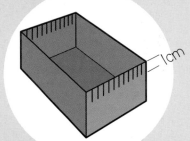
1cm

2 Stick a long piece of string to the edge of the shoebox, next to the first of the cuts.

3 Wrap the string round and round the shoebox so that it slots into the cuts. Tape the end of the string to the box.

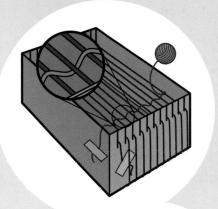

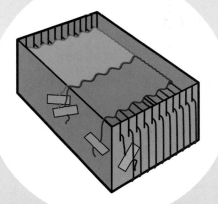

4 Tape a piece of wool to the box. Thread it over the first line of string, under the second, over the third, and so on. When you get to the end of a row, go back the other way.

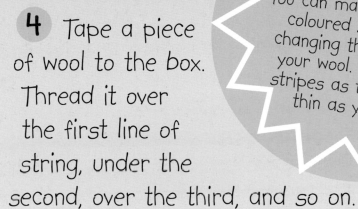
5 When your length of wool runs out, tape the end to the box. Tape another piece of wool to the box where the last piece ended, and carry on.

6 Keep threading wool in and out, and backwards and forwards until you have covered up all the string.

Glossary and Index

bleat   noise made by a sheep

ewe   a mother sheep

lamb   a baby sheep

shearers   people who clip the sheep's fleece

skilled   when a person is very good at doing something

spun   when wool is twisted into long threads

tweed   a type of thick material made from wool

yarn   spun wool that can be used for knitting and weaving

Ideas for teachers and parents

- Make a poster of how yarn is made from the fleece of a sheep and ask the children to illustrate all the different stages, from shearing to cleaning, carding and spinning.

- If you live in or near the countryside, take the children for a walk and look for sheeps' wool caught on fences or brambles. Can you identify breeds of sheep that you see on your walk?

- Make a simple wordsearch, using sheep-related vocabulary from this book.

- If possible, visit a children's farm to see real sheep.

- Research different breeds of sheep and make some factsheets comparing the children's favourite breeds.

- Buy cheeses made from sheep's milk, such as Roquefort and feta, and let the children taste them.

- Make a cottonwool sheep picture. Take a large sheet of paper and ask the children to paint or draw a background of fields and a farm. When the paint has dried, stick cottonwool balls to the background. Take a black marker pen and add heads, legs and other details to turn the cottonwool balls into sheep.

- See how many things you can spot in the home or classroom that have been made using products from sheep.

- Ask the children to collect jokes, stories, poems and rhymes about sheep, and to make up examples of their own.

- Visit **www.david-lewis.com/sheepgame** for a fun online game in which children herd sheep around obstacles and into different pens.

NOTE
Website information is correct at time of going to press. The publishers cannot accept liability for links or information found on third-party websites.